Behind The Wheel™

Jimmie Johnson

NASCAR Driver

Emily Farmer

LOWE'S
48
LOWE'S
MONTE CARLO SS

rosen publishing's
rosen central®

New York

To Michael, who helped me put it all together

Published in 2007 by The Rosen Publishing Group, Inc.
29 East 21st Street, New York, NY 10010

Library of Congress Cataloging-in-Publication Data

Farmer, Emily.
Jimmie Johnson: NASCAR driver / Emily Farmer.—1st ed.
   p. cm.—(Behind the wheel)
Includes bibliographical references and index.
ISBN-13: 978-1-4042-0981-7
ISBN-10: 1-4042-0981-6 (lib. bdg.)
1. Johnson, Jimmie, 1975– 2. Automobile racing drivers—United States—Biography—Juvenile literature.
I. Title. II. Series: Behind the wheel (Rosen Publishing Group)
GV1032.J54F37 2007
796.72092—dc22

                      2006012925
[B]

Manufactured in the United States of America

On the cover: Jimmie Johnson sits behind the wheel of his #48 Lowe's car on April 26, 2006.

CONTENTS

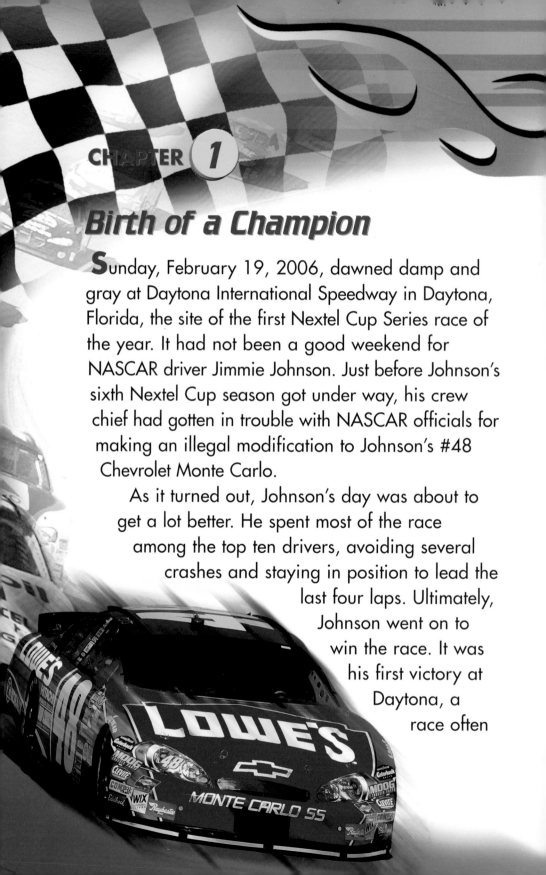

CHAPTER 1

Birth of a Champion

Sunday, February 19, 2006, dawned damp and gray at Daytona International Speedway in Daytona, Florida, the site of the first Nextel Cup Series race of the year. It had not been a good weekend for NASCAR driver Jimmie Johnson. Just before Johnson's sixth Nextel Cup season got under way, his crew chief had gotten in trouble with NASCAR officials for making an illegal modification to Johnson's #48 Chevrolet Monte Carlo.

As it turned out, Johnson's day was about to get a lot better. He spent most of the race among the top ten drivers, avoiding several crashes and staying in position to lead the last four laps. Ultimately, Johnson went on to win the race. It was his first victory at Daytona, a race often

Johnson's #48 Chevrolet leads the pack at the 2006 Daytona 500. The Daytona 500 takes place at Daytona International Speedway in Daytona, Florida. It is the biggest race of the Nextel Cup season.

described as the most important in a NASCAR season. The young driver was well on his way to another spectacular season.

A Racing Family

Jimmie Johnson was born in 1975 in El Cajon, California, to Gary and Cathy Johnson. The Johnson family had a

Jimmie Johnson crosses the finish line during a victory lap celebrating his first-ever Daytona 500 victory on February 19, 2006. The win at Daytona marked Johnson's 19th career Nextel Cup win and started a month-long reign at the top of the points standings.

long history of racing, and it was only natural that Jimmie would follow in their footsteps. He has said that the best thing about racing for him was that his parents always supported what he did. In fact, his mother and father allowed him to race competitively before he even began school.

At the age of four, Jimmie was competing in off-road motorcycle races, or motocross, at Southern California racetracks. By the time he was eight years old, he had won his first motocross championship. It would be the first of many championships to come.

Jimmie's grandparents owned a motorcycle shop in El Cajon, and his father, who had also raced motorcycles, worked there as a mechanic. When he wasn't working in the shop, Jimmie's father volunteered at a local motorcycle track. He helped build the tracks while Jimmie's mother worked at the concession stand. Before long, Jimmie would be racing on those very tracks.

As he entered his early teens, Jimmie was drawn away from motocross by a combination of injury and opportunity. The fact that he had suffered broken bones racing worried his mother. She was afraid that Jimmie could get seriously hurt, or even killed, by racing motocross. At the same time, his father had started working in a garage for the Mickey Thompson Entertainment Group, which did stadium car racing. Jimmie's father managed to get him off the motorcycle and into a car, which put Cathy's mind at ease. It also gave her son a new challenge to work on.

From Two Wheels to Four

At age 15, Jimmie Johnson became the youngest driver to race in the Mickey Thompson Stadium Off-Road Series. He debuted in the Superlite competition and began to make a name for himself. Over the next few years, Jimmie competed in the Short-Course Off-Road Drivers Association (SODA), the Micky Thompson Entertainment Group (MTEG) Stadium Series, and the

Short Course Off-Road Enthusiasts (SCORE) International. Jimmie did extremely well in these small racing leagues, recording more than 25 wins and 100 top-three finishes. He also won Rookie of the Year in all three.

Competing in three different leagues exposed Jimmie to a lot of different racing styles. In SODA races, Jimmie had the opportunity to drive trucks, modified buggies, and cars that were based on the Volkswagen Beetle. Most of the SODA races were held in Wisconsin, with the highlight of the series being the Crandon International Off-Road Raceway championship event.

In the MTEG Superlite competition, Jimmie was driving a very different sort of vehicle. A superlite is an open-wheel vehicle, meaning the wheels are positioned outside the main body of the car. Open-wheel cars are also seen in Formula One racing, the Indy Racing League (IRL), and a number of other types of events. They are different from NASCAR vehicles, which are closed-wheel cars. Superlites have an open cockpit and very little sheet metal covering the frame of the car, making them more like buggies than a conventional car.

In SCORE International, Jimmie found his niche. This off-road series, which includes both motocross and truck events, puts on a number of races in the deserts in and around Jimmie's native California. Jimmie won a championship in the SCORE desert series in 1993 before moving on to a SCORE stadium truck series in 1994.

Johnson's early career included driving buggies much like this one. Johnson returned to his off-road roots in the Race of Champions' Nations Cup as a rally driver for the United States in 2002 and 2004.

Another championship came his way in 1995 when he won the Superlite title.

Getting Noticed

Back in 1993, Jimmie's mentor, champion supercross racer Rick Johnson, introduced him to Herb Fishel. Fishel was the executive director of GM Racing. After watching Jimmie race, Fishel was impressed with the young man's behavior both on and off the track. Besides being a good driver, Jimmie was also active when it came to managing his own career.

Being a NASCAR driver is about more than just driving. Throughout his career, Johnson has earned praise and comparisons to team-mate Jeff Gordon for his ability to be poised and confident when dealing with the media.

Jimmie Johnson put together an impressive string of victories over the next few years. The young phenom won six championships in various off-road series, including three Mickey Thompson Stadium Truck Series championships from 1992 to 1994. He also won a SCORE Desert championship in 1994, and SODA Winter Series championships in 1996 and 1997.

Between all these wins, Jimmie also found time to provide commentary for ESPN when the network covered SODA in the mid-1990s. When a television network shows a sporting event, there are usually two people who talk during the event to let viewers know what's going on: the play-by-play announcer and the color commentator. The play-by-play announcer gives a factual description of what's taking place, while the color commentator provides background information about the sport, the participants, and their strategies. Jimmie was the color commentator for the events. During

Drivers in the Busch Series 1999 Hot Wheels.com 300 race at Homestead-Miami Speedway on November 13. The Busch Series is a training ground for stock-car racing's biggest stage—the Nextel Cup.

this time, Jimmie met Stan and Randy Herzog, who were impressed with his abilities. The Herzog brothers were part owners of Herzog Jackson Motorsports. Founded in 1987, the company was involved in a lot of different racing series, including SODA, the American Speed Association (ASA), and the NASCAR Busch Series.

Jimmie and the Herzogs went to talk to Fishel. Together, the three men teamed up to put Jimmie in an ASA car in 1997. This was the first time Jimmie raced professionally on pavement, which was a big difference from battling it out in the mud, sand, and dirt of off-road racing. Although he raced in only three events that year, it was another major step in his career.

Out of the Mud

Quickly making the adjustment to the smooth tracks and the close contact with other drivers, Jimmie got his first two stock-car wins the very next year. In 1998, he competed in a full ASA season, driving the #44 Chevrolet for Herzog. He finished fourth in the ASA points race and was named ASA Rookie of the Year.

The ASA puts on a number of different events, many of which were nationally televised. A number of NASCAR drivers got their start in the ASA, including Matt Kenseth, Mark Martin, and Rusty Wallace. When Jimmie came to the ASA, he wanted to learn as much as he could about his new environment. Since he was racing for Herzog on a team based out of Milwaukee, Wisconsin, he moved to Milwaukee. Living there allowed Jimmie to spend a lot of time with his crew chief, Howie Lettow, and familiarize himself with the car he would be driving.

In 1999, Jimmie started in five Busch Series races. He finished third in the ASA points race and won two ASA races, at Memphis Motorsports Park in Memphis, Alabama, and at Orange County Speedway near Rougemont, North Carolina.

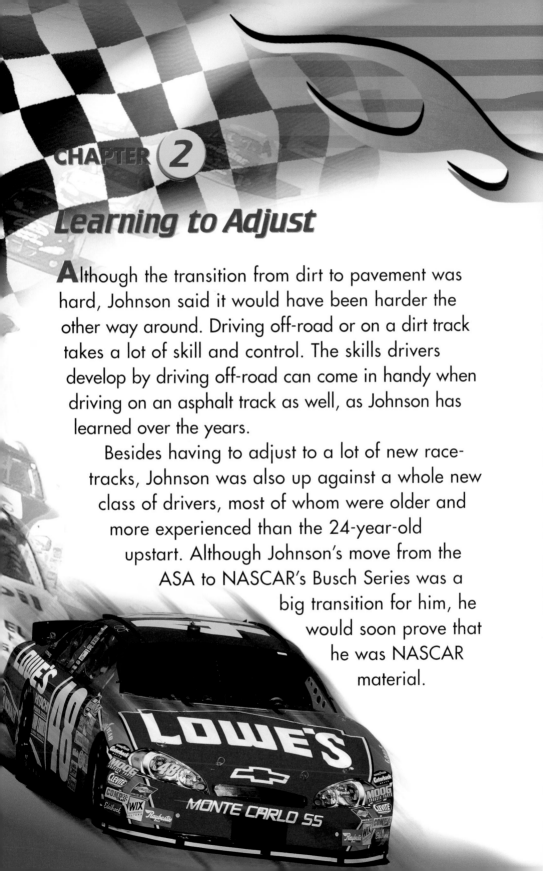

Learning to Adjust

Although the transition from dirt to pavement was hard, Johnson said it would have been harder the other way around. Driving off-road or on a dirt track takes a lot of skill and control. The skills drivers develop by driving off-road can come in handy when driving on an asphalt track as well, as Johnson has learned over the years.

Besides having to adjust to a lot of new race-tracks, Johnson was also up against a whole new class of drivers, most of whom were older and more experienced than the 24-year-old upstart. Although Johnson's move from the ASA to NASCAR's Busch Series was a big transition for him, he would soon prove that he was NASCAR material.

In what would become a legendary NASCAR moment, Donnie Allison's #1 car crashes with Cale Yarborough's #11 car during the last lap of the 1979 Daytona 500. Fans all across the United States watched this crash during what was the first live television broadcast of an entire stock-car race.

What Is NASCAR?

The National Association for Stock Car Racing, or NASCAR, was established in 1948 in Wilkes County, North Carolina. NASCAR sanctions three major race series that drivers compete in: the Nextel Cup, the Busch Series, and the Craftsman Truck Series.

The Nextel Cup, formerly known as the Winston Cup, is the largest series in NASCAR. The Daytona 500, the biggest event in the Nextel Cup Series, starts the season in February. The season ends at Homestead-Miami Speedway in November. In between these two races, drivers travel the country to compete in 36 races at 22 different racetracks, each with its own unique characteristics.

Some people consider the Busch Series a place for young drivers to learn the ropes before competing in the Nextel Cup. However, many drivers compete in both the Busch and the Nextel Cup series. A driver can race in the Busch Series on Saturday and then race in the Nextel Cup Series on Sunday, on the very same racetrack.

Paying Dues

Before they are qualified to compete in the Busch Series, drivers usually hone their skills by racing in other divisions. Someone who has had success at a local stock-car racetrack can advance to a touring division, as Johnson eventually did, doing short-track racing. Short-track competitions are generally rough-and-tumble events. Drivers race in close quarters, and since the track is so short, the cars are turning almost constantly. Most short-track races result in a lot of bumping and scraping between the cars, but they're good training for up-and-coming racers, who have to learn quickly how to handle themselves in tense situations. Some short-track divisions include the Dodge Weekly Series, the AutoZone Elite division, the Busch North and West series, and the Featherlite Modified Series. Drivers compete in these divisions to gain experience and work their way up to the Nextel Cup Series.

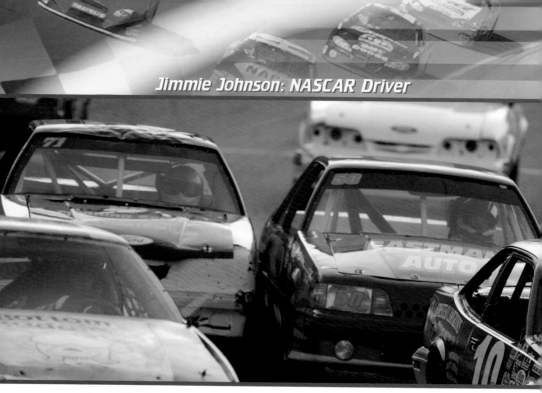

A tight pack of street stock-division race cars jockey for position on the Thunder Road racetrack in Barre, Vermont, on August 27, 2004. Tracks such as Thunder Road provide opportunities for young drivers across the country to get used to life on the track.

Most young people who want to be NASCAR drivers start out racing stock cars and gradually move up the ranks, but that's not quite how Jimmie Johnson did it. He started out with his first love, motorcycles, and eventually made his way around to cars. By doing so, he found his own way to be successful.

Milestones

Things continued to improve for Johnson in 2000. He went even further in the Busch Series, finishing tenth in the points standings and coming in third for the Busch Series Rookie of the Year Award. He finished sixth in three races, at South Boston Speedway, Michigan International Speedway, and Homestead-Miami Speedway. He also qualified to start fourth at Darlington Raceway, in South Carolina—the best start of his career.

The year 2001 saw two major milestones for Johnson. He earned his first Busch Series win and raced in his first Nextel Cup Series event. Later that year, on October 7, he made his Nextel Cup Series debut at Lowe's Motor Speedway in Charlotte, North Carolina. He qualified for the race in 15th place, and finished 39th, driving for a new owner—Hendrick Motorsports.

Young Guns

When Johnson was signed to drive for Hendrick Motorsports in 2001, it was big news for NASCAR. Johnson was considered by many to be a racing prodigy, and fans were impressed with how quickly he had moved up through the ranks. Johnson had been driving in the Busch Series for Herzog Jackson Motorsports, but in July 2000, the team's main sponsor, Alltel, announced it would not sponsor the team for the following year. When word got out that Johnson might be looking to make a change, he began getting offers from all over.

Johnson wasn't sure what to do, so he decided to ask Jeff Gordon for advice. Gordon was another young driver who had become incredibly successful. The two ran into each other before a Busch Series race in

After winning the 2002 NAPA Auto Parts 500, Jimmie Johnson shows off his trophy while flanked by team owners Rick Hendrick *(left)* and Jeff Gordon *(right)*. The race took place at the California Speedway in Fontana, California, located about an hour away from Johnson's hometown of El Cajon.

2000, and Johnson asked to speak to Gordon before the race. But before Johnson could ask him for any advice, Gordon surprised him by asking if he would be interested in joining Gordon on the Hendrick Motorsports team.

Gordon said the company was planning to add a new Winston Cup team, and that they were interested in Johnson. About a month later, the deal was done and Johnson had signed a contract. He would be Gordon's teammate, competing for the biggest prize in stock-car racing: the Winston Cup.

SPONSORS

Perhaps more than in any other sport, sponsorships play a large role in racing. When a business sponsors a racing team, it pays to have its name and its logo associated with that team. This means the business's name will be on that team's cars, on the drivers' clothes, and on products like T-shirts, hats, and model cars. It also means the drivers will do in-store appearances, commercials, and other promotions. Jimmie Johnson drives the #48 Lowe's car and travels all over the country to appear at Lowe's stores.

Drivers don't just have one sponsor—they have dozens. That's why their cars and clothes are covered with so many logos. The reason why drivers need all these sponsors is simple: It can cost tens of millions of dollars to maintain a NASCAR team, and that number is getting bigger every year. When NASCAR got started, most of the sponsors had something to do with racing, such as Pennzoil motor oil, NAPA auto parts, and other car-related products. But as NASCAR became more popular, more businesses got involved. Today, companies such as UPS, Cingular Wireless, and Jimmie Johnson's main sponsor, Lowe's, sponsor NASCAR teams.

A Legacy in the Making

The owner of Hendrick Motorsports, Rick Hendrick, became a Winston Cup Series team owner in 1984. His team won four championships between 1995 and 1998 with drivers Terry Labonte and Jeff Gordon.

It was big news when Johnson joined the Hendrick team to be Gordon's teammate. Gordon had become a superstar when he entered the Winston Cup about ten years earlier. People saw some of Gordon's talent in Johnson and were looking forward to seeing what these two talented drivers could do together as teammates.

Although the Hendrick team was glad to have Johnson on board, no one was quite sure what to think of him as he entered the 2002 season. People were waiting to find out if he would measure up to the potential he had shown. After all, he was still very young and didn't have a lot of experience in stock-car racing. He would also be racing against some of the best drivers in the country. Still, everything seemed to be coming together for Johnson. He was on a great team, and everyone was watching to see what would happen.

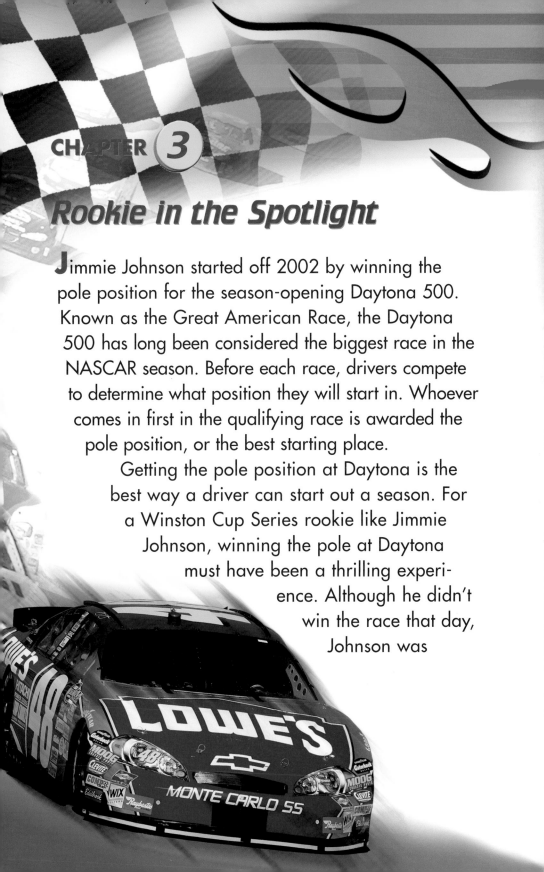

CHAPTER 3

Rookie in the Spotlight

Jimmie Johnson started off 2002 by winning the pole position for the season-opening Daytona 500. Known as the Great American Race, the Daytona 500 has long been considered the biggest race in the NASCAR season. Before each race, drivers compete to determine what position they will start in. Whoever comes in first in the qualifying race is awarded the pole position, or the best starting place.

Getting the pole position at Daytona is the best way a driver can start out a season. For a Winston Cup Series rookie like Jimmie Johnson, winning the pole at Daytona must have been a thrilling experience. Although he didn't win the race that day, Johnson was

A green flag signals the start of the 2002 Daytona 500. The double line of cars is led by Jimmie Johnson's #48 Chevrolet Monte Carlo. Johnson would ultimately finish the race in 15th place.

clearly off to a promising start, and all eyes were on him.

An Impressive Start

Halfway through the season, Johnson was in third place in the points standings. This was an impressive achievement for a relative rookie who had raced in only three cup series races before the 2002 season.

Johnson drew a lot of attention to himself with his late-season win at the Dover International Speedway in Delaware. His victory at Dover put him in the points lead, a first for a rookie. With only a handful of races left in the season, Johnson was still a contender. Going into the October 27 race at the Atlanta Motor Speedway, it looked like he had a shot at the championship.

Unfortunately, it was not meant to be. Johnson suffered a major setback when a member of his pit crew was hit by another driver. He and his crew made sure that the man was all right, which set him back significantly in the race. At the next race, Johnson fought his way from the back of the pack, only to suffer mechanical problems. He finished in 37th place, hurting his chances for the championship. Johnson closed out the season with an overall rank of fifth.

Jimmie Johnson had what anyone would consider an excellent rookie season. In fact, he came in second for

Johnson's #48 car moves down the straightaway at Dover International Speedway on September 22, 2002. The short, one-mile track is located in Dover, Delaware, and is nicknamed the Monster Mile. Johnson won the race, making it his second win at Dover and the third win of his rookie season.

Rookie of the Year honors, trailing Ryan Newman by only a handful of points. Johnson's three wins for the season might not sound like a lot, but in NASCAR, it's not bad—especially considering that he had more than 20 finishes in the top ten during that first year. He spent nearly the entire season in the top ten of the points standings, finishing fifth overall.

Adding It Up

In NASCAR, earning points is almost more important than winning or losing. NASCAR championships are determined based on how many points a driver has accumulated throughout the season.

Drivers and owners each earn points from each race. Owners earn points for each race in which any of their drivers compete. Drivers, naturally enough, earn points only when they drive. The points they earn are based on where they finish and how they do in the race.

With his fifth-place finish the year before, it's safe to say Johnson was feeling good as he went into the 2003 season. The young rookie had proved himself to be a real competitor. Johnson continued to improve, scoring more points, racking up more top-ten finishes, and winning three races. He also won the All-Star Challenge at his sponsor's home track, Lowe's Motor Speedway. Although no points are awarded for the All-Star Challenge, it is a great honor to even be eligible to compete in the event. Only 20 of the season's best drivers are picked to enter the challenge.

Despite a few rough races early in the season, Johnson managed to stay in the top ten of the points standings for the whole season. An accident at Dover, a track where he had won both races the year before, frustrated Johnson: he lost control of his car on the 278th lap and crashed against a barrier after striking a wall. Despite this setback, he spent the latter part of the season in the top five.

Driver Safety

Accidents like the one Johnson had at Dover are all too common in NASCAR. Because accidents happen so

Jimmie Johnson is suited up for a practice session at Phoenix International Raceway in Phoenix, Arizona. Johnson's protective gear covers him from head to toe. If it weren't for his sponsors' logos on his helmet and jumpsuit, it would be impossible to tell who is behind the wheel.

frequently, NASCAR is always working to make its races safer. The stock cars NASCAR drivers use have all the safety features you would expect—and then some.

For example, the frame of the car is reinforced with a roll cage, a structure of strong metal tubes that sits inside the frame and stabilizes it. In a crash, the roll cage keeps the driver from being crushed. The driver's seat is engineered to protect his body and keep him strapped in. Rather than a regular seat belt, NASCAR drivers have belts fastened around their legs and shoulders. This method of strapping the driver in is designed to keep him safe and stable.

Before they even get in their cars, drivers put on other equipment to protect themselves. All drivers wear

Jimmie Johnson has said the worst crash of his career was during a Busch Series race at Watkins Glen in 2000, when his brakes failed, and he crashed through the wall. Fortunately, it was a "soft" wall, designed to absorb the shock of impact. Johnson thinks the soft wall may have saved his life.

Besides the soft walls, Johnson's #48 Chevrolet has other safety features to keep him on the track. One of the most important devices is called a restrictor plate. This device reduces a stock car's speed by limiting the amount of air and fuel that enter the car's engine. NASCAR requires the use of restrictor plates at certain racetracks where cars can otherwise go too fast and lose control. Fortunately for Johnson, he has been very successful at restrictor plate races.

Johnson's car, as required by NASCAR, also features roof flaps. Introduced in 1994, the small flaps help catch air and put downward pressure on the car so it doesn't flip up into the air at high speeds.

helmets, which have multiple layers to absorb shocks. The brightly colored jumpsuits drivers wear aren't just a good place to show off their sponsors—the suits are fireproof as well.

In 2001, Dale Earnhardt, one of NASCAR's greatest drivers, was killed in a crash. He died from injuries to his head and neck. At the time, a lot of drivers were considering the use of head and neck support (HANS) devices. A HANS is like a sturdy collar that keeps the driver's head in place to protect it in case of a crash. After Earnhardt's crash, NASCAR decided all drivers have to use an approved device that keeps their head and neck stable.

Soft walls are the last line of defense to protect drivers if there is a crash. Most NASCAR racetracks used to have walls of solid concrete, but NASCAR engineers created walls to absorb some of the force of a high-speed crash. They came up with a few different ideas, using things like foam and rubber, and began trying out the walls at various racetracks. Now soft walls can be found nearly everywhere.

A Shot at the Championship

As the 2003 season drew to a close, Johnson found himself within striking distance of winning it all. He was trying to best another young up-and-coming driver, Matt Kenseth, who had the points lead going into the last race of the season at Homestead-Miami Speedway. It looked like Johnson had his chance when the engine of Kenseth's car blew, but he failed to earn enough points to take the lead from his opponent. If the 2003 season had been run under the points system introduced in 2004, Johnson would have won the championship. Instead, he finished in third place. Rather than dwell on his loss, Johnson looked ahead to the future—the 2004 season.

A New Points System

Up until 2004, the points system was structured in such a way that a single driver could earn so many points that it would be mathematically impossible for anyone to catch up with him. A lot of people felt this made the end of the season less exciting.

Starting in 2004, the Winston Cup got a new sponsor— Nextel Communications. The Winston Cup Series became known as the Nextel Cup Series, and NASCAR decided to alter its points system to keep things more competitive. After the first 26 races of the season, the top ten drivers are now "locked in" to compete for the championship. The points these drivers have built up during the season are wiped out, and they are assigned new points. Under this system, any of these drivers have a good chance of winning the Nextel Cup, which puts some excitement back into the end of the season.

Grace Under Pressure

The 2004 season had its ups and downs for Johnson. His season began with a disappointing 16th place finish at Las Vegas. A collision at Rockingham with driver Kent Schrader made it so Johnson couldn't finish the race. He managed to get a win at Darlington just a couple of weeks later and strung together some more top-ten finishes over the next few months. Going into the last ten races of the season, Johnson was in first place with a comfortable lead of more than 200 points. It looked like he was on track to win the championship that had eluded him the year before.

However, Johnson and his team may have gotten too comfortable. He and his crew chief, Chad Knaus, made some adjustments to his car that proved to be detrimental. Engine failures during his next three races, at Indianapolis, Watkins Glen, and Michigan, caused Johnson to place nearly last in each race, losing a lot of points. By making changes to his car, Johnson and Knaus were taking the kind of risk that is common in NASCAR. Each race is different, and drivers work with their pit crews to adjust their car to the track and the conditions. By doing so, they hope to gain an advantage over the competition.

Although he and his crew managed to recover, it was difficult for him to make up the points he had lost. Still, he clearly wasn't going to give up, and he stayed in contention for the championship right up to the end. Johnson

Jimmie Johnson's pit crew gets to work during the DirectTV 500 at Martinsville Speedway in Martinsville, Virginia, on April 2, 2006. Johnson's crew is headed by his crew chief, Chad Knaus.

won four of his last six races and finished in the top ten in all of them.

Just when Johnson and his crew were recovering from their struggles, they learned that a terrible tragedy had taken place. On October 24, a plane carrying members of the Hendrick family crashed in Virginia. Ten people were killed, including Rick Hendrick's brother, son, and nieces.

The pit crew is a group of mechanics and specialists who make sure the driver's car is in the best shape it can be for a race. The pit crew is led by a crew chief, who gets the car ready for each race. The crew chief also makes decisions during the race about what the team should do.

You can see the pit crew working during the race when the driver makes a pit stop. Each member of the crew has a specific job to do, like Mike Trower, Johnson's front tire changer, and Chris Anderson, the "jackman," who is responsible for using a jack to elevate the car so its tires can be changed.

Some of the crew's most important work comes before the race. When drivers arrive at a track, they must drive qualifying laps to see who will get the pole position for the start of the race. The qualifying lap allows each driver to work with his pit crew to make sure his car is at its best for that particular race.

Johnson has to pay attention to the car during qualifying so he can tell crew chief Chad Knaus and the rest of the pit crew if anything needs attention. Depending on Johnson's feedback, Knaus may decide to use a different set of tires or adjust the engine. This can help Johnson do better during the race.

Johnson and his team were devastated. But rather than allowing this tragedy to hurt his team, Johnson was motivated to try even harder. He won his next race, at Atlanta, and dedicated the race to the victims of the crash.

Just like the year before, Johnson's season would be decided at Homestead. This time, his rival was Kurt Busch, who led Johnson by only 18 points going into the race. A win for Johnson would almost certainly get him the championship—as long as Kurt Busch came in second place or lower, without leading any laps. Despite Johnson's best efforts, it was not meant to be. He came in second, and Busch won the cup by only eight points.

Victory and Defeat

Johnson ended 2004 on a personal high note by getting married to model Chandra Janway in December, and things were looking up as he entered the 2005 season. He had his first win of the season at Las Vegas and finished in the top ten for his first eight races. He spent the whole year in the top five of the points standings. A victory at Dover and two more at Lowe's Motor Speedway made for four straight wins at his sponsor's track. His win at Dover was his best performance of the year. He led 134 of the course's 404 laps, which pushed him into first place in the points standings.

The August race at Bristol Motor Speedway in Bristol, Tennessee, is the last race before the points cutoff is established for the Race for the Nextel Cup. This makes for some extremely competitive racing, and the short, steeply banked track sees a lot of accidents. Johnson didn't crash at Bristol, but his engine broke down and he wasn't able to finish the race.

Although Johnson recovered from Bristol to win at Dover, that didn't mean everything was going perfectly. The next week, at Talladega, Johnson was involved in a six-car accident. In the 20th lap of the race, Johnson hit Elliott Sadler's car, causing it to spin out. Mark Martin, Dale Earnhardt Jr., Michael Waltrip, and Mike Skinner were also involved in the crash. The crash caused Johnson to finish 31st and lose his points lead.

Back to Homestead

It was the same story again for Johnson in 2005: his season would be determined by his performance at Homestead. The points leader going into the race was Tony Stewart. On the 126th lap of the race, one of Johnson's tires blew out and he hit the wall. The accident put him in 40th place in the race, and he finished 5th in points.

Johnson had lost big races before, but this loss hit him hard. His chances of winning the 2005 Nextel Cup had been better than ever before. Despite his disappointment, Johnson chose to look forward to his next season with hope instead of thinking about the past.

Jimmie Johnson collides with Elliott Sadler's #38 car during the UAW-Ford 500 at the Talladega Superspeedway in Talladega, Alabama, on October 2, 2005. Mark Martin, Dale Earnhardt Jr., Michael Waltrip, and Mike Skinner were also caught up in the crash, which caused Johnson to finish the race in a disappointing 31st place.

The 2006 season started off great for Johnson with a win at Daytona, a race that many drivers dream of winning. Johnson led the race for 24 laps, showing that he is truly a contender and ranks among the great NASCAR drivers of the present day.

CHAPTER 4

Out of the Driver's Seat

When he's not racing, Johnson likes to spend time with his family. He enjoys listening to country music and alternative rock, following the stock market, and eating steak and seafood dinners. He also enjoys spending time in the water, on a boat or jet ski, or in the mountains, bicycling or snowboarding.

Johnson is married to Chandra Janway, a former model. Chandra was introduced to Johnson by Jeff Gordon in 2002. The couple got married in December 2004 and took a ski-trip honeymoon for New Year's. Although not as outspoken as some of his fellow drivers, Johnson is not shy. He has tried his hand at acting and got his first role in the 2004 NASCAR/IMAX film *IMAX*

Jimmie and Chandra celebrate Johnson's win at the Sylvania 300 on September 14, 2003, at New Hampshire International Speedway in Loudon, New Hampshire. It was Johnson's third win of the season. Now married, the couple dated for a few years before tying the knot in 2004.

NASCAR 3-D. Johnson and his crew chief, Chad Knaus, also made an appearance in an episode of the television show *Las Vegas*, playing themselves, in 2006.

Although he and his family live in Charlotte, North Carolina, home to many NASCAR drivers, owners, and mechanics, Johnson is still a California boy at heart. When asked about his favorite restaurants, Johnson listed In-N-Out Burger, a California fast-food chain, and a Mexican food stand in his native El Cajon.

Johnson is a hometown hero in El Cajon. The local newspaper, the *San Diego Union-Tribune*, features stories on his visits back home. Johnson received a standing ovation while attending a San Diego Padres baseball game, and he co-owns a nearby Chevrolet dealership with Rick Hendrick.

In 2006, Jimmie and Chandra established the Jimmie Johnson Foundation. The foundation benefits five charities that help children: the American Red Cross, Victory Junction Gang, Randy Dorton Memorial Fund, Make-A-Wish, and the Hendrick Marrow Program.

Changes for the Future

One of the biggest challenges Johnson faces in the future will be adjusting to driving an entirely new kind of car. By 2009, all NASCAR drivers will be driving "the car of tomorrow," a new model of stock car with a lot of additional safety features. The difference between the car of tomorrow and a present-day stock

Media, fans, and officials surround Johnson and his #48 Chevrolet as he shows off the Harley J. Earl trophy. The trophy signals Johnson's 2006 Daytona 500 win.

The #48 Chevrolet is framed by Jimmie Johnson's team as they fill Victory Lane to celebrate his win at the 2006 Daytona 500. Johnson's success depends on the hard work of a lot of people, who together make all of his victories possible.

car will be space. The area where the driver sits will be bigger, so there can be more padding around him. One important place for padding will be on the driver's door, where there will be a protective "crush zone." The padding around the driver's neck will also be thicker.

In the front and back of the car, the bumpers will be adjusted to help keep the car stable on the racetrack. The exhaust system will be altered as well. Rather than running under the driver's seat, the exhaust will run through the frame and out the right-hand side of the car. Overall, the car of tomorrow will put together a lot of safety elements that have been developed over the years and bring in new technology to keep all the drivers safer.

Looking Ahead

Jimmie Johnson has been racing since he was a young boy. From his days traveling around California with his parents to his current life as a famous race car driver, flying across the country to compete at some of the biggest races in the world, Johnson has been successful at nearly everything he has set out to do.

Almost every year Jimmie Johnson has competed in the Nextel Cup Series, people said he had a good chance of winning it all. Although he may have felt frustrated by his losses, he has many years of great racing ahead of him.

Everyone agrees that Johnson is an incredibly talented driver. Throughout his career, he has exceeded people's expectations of him, and with hard work and a good team behind him, he is sure to succeed at his ultimate goal—winning a Nextel Cup championship.

Awards

1991 Mickey Thompson Entertainment Group Superlite Rookie of the Year

1992 MTEG Stadium Racing Series champion
Miller Challenge Outdoor Series Rookie of the Year

1993 MTEG Stadium Racing Series champion

1994 MTEG Stadium Racing Series champion
SCORE Desert champion

1995 SCORE Class 8/Trophy Truck Rookie of the Year

1996 SODA Winter Series champion

1997 SODA Winter Series champion

1998 Pat Schauer Memorial ASA Rookie of the Year

2002 Race of Champions Nations Cup (with Jeff Gordon and Colin Edwards)

2004 Sporting News Driver of the Year

2006 Daytona 500 winner

Glossary

bank The angle of a racetrack; NASCAR tracks are banked on the turns to keep cars from losing traction.

crew chief The leader of the pit crew.

frame The steel structure around which a car is built.

lap One trip around a racetrack.

motocross A combination of the words "motorcycle" and "cross-country," motocross is a type of motorcycle racing done on natural, outdoor tracks.

Nextel Cup The most prestigious NASCAR event; formerly known as the Winston Cup.

phenom Slang term used to refer to a very talented or skilled person; short for phenomenon.

pole The best starting position in a race; a driver has pole position if he has the best qualifying time.

prodigy A young person with an extraordinary talent or skill.

restrictor plate A device that slows down a car by restricting the flow of air and fuel to the carburetor.

roll cage A steel frame that protects the driver during a crash.

short track A track that is shorter than 1 mile (1.6 km).

sponsor A person or a business that pays a track, team, or driver to advertise itself.

stock car A race car that is similar to a standard retail car.

For More Information

Hendrick Motorsports
4400 Papa Joe Hendrick Boulevard
Charlotte, NC 28262
(704) 455-0324
Web site: http://hendrickmotorsports.com

Jimmie Johnson Fan Club
P.O. Box 5599
Mooresville, NC 28027
(800) 338-6016
Web site: http://www.jimmiejohnson.com

NASCAR
P.O. Box 2875
Daytona Beach, FL 32120
(386) 253-0611
Web site: http://www.nascar.com

SCORE International
23961 Craftsman Road #A
Calabasas, CA 91302
(818) 225-8402
Web site: http://www.score-international.com

Web Sites

Due to the changing nature of Internet links, Rosen Publishing has developed an online list of Web sites related to the subject of this book. This site is updated regularly. Please use this link to access the list:

http://www.rosenlinks.com/bw/jijo

For Further Reading

Buckley, James. *NASCAR*. New York, NY: DK Children, 2005.

Fielden, Greg. *NASCAR Chronicle*. Lincolnwood, IL: Publications International, 2005.

Fresina, Michael. *For the Love of NASCAR: An A-to-Z Primer for NASCAR Fans of All Ages*. Chicago, IL: Triumph Books, 2005.

Gilden, Mel. *NASCAR Racers: How They Work*. New York, NY: HarperEntertainment, 2000.

Martin, Mark, and Beth Tuschak. *NASCAR for Dummies*. Hoboken, NJ: Wiley Publishing Inc., 2005.

NASCAR. *Official NASCAR Trivia*. New York, NY: Harper Collins, 1998.

Schaefer, A. R. *The History of NASCAR*. Mankato, MN: Capstone Press, 2005.

Stevens, Josh. *Jimmie Johnson: NASCAR's Top Drivers of 2004*. St. Louis, MO: Reedy Press, 2005.

Woods, Bob. *Pit Pass: Behind the Scenes of NASCAR*. Pleasantville, NY: Reader's Digest Children's Books, 2005.

Young, Jesse. *Stock Cars*. Minneapolis, MN: Capstone Press, 1995.

Bibliography

Center, Bill. "Johnson Building Early Momentum." SignsonSanDiego.com. February 27, 2006. Retrieved February 2006 (http://www. signonsandiego.com/sports/20060227-9999-1s27carside.html).

Finney, Mike. "Jimmie Johnson Isn't Panicking." February 26, 2004. Retrieved February 2006 (http://www.jimmiejohnson48.com/ modules.php?name=Content&pa=showpage&pid=117).

James, Brant. "Desert Zoom." *St. Petersburg Times* online. February 15, 2004. Retrieved February 2006 (http://www.sptimes.com/2004/ 02/15/Sports/Desert_zoom.shtml).

James, Brant. "Johnson's Rally Comes Up .342 Seconds Short." *St. Petersburg Times* Online. November 22, 2004. Retrieved February 2006 (http://www.sptimes.com/2004/11/22/Sports/ Johnson_s_rally_comes.shtml).

Lemasters, Ron, Jr., et. al. *Jimmie Johnson: A Desert Rat's Race to NASCAR Stardom*. St. Paul, MN: Motorbooks International, 2004.

Montgomery, Lee. "In Review: J. Johnson." NASCAR.com. December 22, 2004. Retrieved February 2006 (http://www.nascar.com/2004/ news/headlines/cup/12/22/jjohnson_review).

NASCAR. "Jimmie Johnson." February 9, 2006. Retrieved February 2006 (http://www.nascar.com/news/headlines/cup/ johnson.bio/index.html).

NASCAR. "Johnson: Title Will Ease 2004 Disappointment." January 22, 2005. Retrieved February 2006 (http://www.nascar.com/2005/ news/headlines/cup/01/22/bc.car.nascar.daytonate.ap/ index.html).

NASCAR. "Q&A: Jimmie Johnson." April 28, 2004. Retrieved February 2006 (http://www.nascar.com/2004/news/headlines/official/ 04/28/jjohnson_qa/index.html).

"No. 48 Jimmie Johnson." The Inside Groove. 2006. Retrieved February 2006 (http://www.theinsidegroove.com/drivers/ driver_info.php4?driver=Jimmie%20Johnson).

The Official NASCAR Handbook: Everything You Want to Know About the NASCAR Winston Cup Series. New York, NY: HarperCollins Publishers, 1998.

Index

About the Author

Originally from Oregon, Emily Farmer works as an editor at the *Daily Star* newspaper in Oneonta, New York. An avid baseball fan, she became exposed to NASCAR through friends and co-workers. When she's not watching a race or a game, Emily enjoys gardening, fixing up her house, and knitting.

Photo Credits

Cover, p. 40 © Rusty Jarrett/Getty Images for NASCAR; pp. 1, 6, 26, 39 © Jonathan Ferrey/Getty Images; pp. 5, 24 © Chris Stanford/Getty Images; p. 9 © Jacques Brinon/AP; p. 10 © Alan Diaz/AP; p. 11© David Taylor/Allsport/Getty Images Sport; p. 14 © AP Photo/Ric Feld, Stringer; p. 16 © AP Photo/Toby Talbot; p. 18 © Robert Laberge/Getty Images; p. 22 © AP Photo/David Graham; p. 31 © Nick Laham/Getty Images; p. 35 © AP Photo/Greg Suvino; p. 37 © Darrell Ingham/Getty Images.

Designer: Gene Mollica